THE END GAME

*A Training Guide for Those Who Truly
Want to End Sexual Harassment*

Julie Still-Rolin

The End Game: A Training Guide for Those Who Truly Want to End Sexual Harassment
© 2017 by Julie Still-Rolin.
All Rights Reserved.

All rights reserved. No part of this book may be reproduced in any form or by any electronic or mechanical means including information storage and retrieval systems, without permission in writing from the author. The only exception is by a reviewer, who may quote short excerpts in a review.

Cover designed by Kindle Direct Publishing

This book is a work of fiction. Names, characters, places, and incidents either are products of the author's imagination or are used fictitiously. Any resemblance to actual persons, living or dead, events, or locales is entirely coincidental.

Julie Still-Rolin
Visit my website at www.sexualharassmentguru.com

Printed in the United States of America

First Printing: Aug 2017
Kindle Direct Publishing

Gender equality is more than a goal in itself. It is a precondition for meeting the challenge of reducing poverty, promoting sustainable development and building good governance.
—KOFI ANNAN

Dedicated to my wife for supporting and believing in my dreams, my children for inspiring me to push forward, and my fellow victims and advocates against sexual harassment and violence.

INTRODUCTION

THIS PROJECT'S OBJECTIVE is this: to take steps toward putting an end to sexual harassment. After experiencing sexual harassment, I needed to understand it. Sexual harassment is complex because of its relationship to power and its intertwining with gender and equality. To simply define sexual harassment as unwanted advances, touching, etc. is insufficient. This is one reason why training fails. Einstein said that if he was given one hour to solve a problem, he would spend 55 minutes defining it. In order to truly solve the problem of sexual harassment, we must first understand the problem completely.

The current United States president's admission of and dismissal of the significance of his statement, "Grab 'em by the pussy. You can do anything," demonstrates the ever-progressive need to prevent and handle sexual harassment. However, more and more organizations and institutions are turning to low cost online training. I have taken online sexual harassment training. It is a joke. I clicked through the slides and ended up with a simple test that anyone could answer without even having gone through the information. Other forms of training are often impersonal and therefore ineffective. Pedagogical theories have illustrated that lectures followed by tests are not efficient means of instruction. So, why are we still using this method to teach sexual harassment training? As an educator, I studied effective pedagogical techniques, and as a solutions developer, I employ these methods for more effective training.

The abundance of information in today's society can often lead to a lack of knowledge. Bits and pieces do not lead to a whole understanding. Understanding sexual harassment requires an examination of the issue in entirety. This means looking at the motivations of the harasser, the personality types associated with these motivations, and the ways to identify these proactively. Understanding the victims of sexual harassment is also important. Although anyone is subject to become a victim of sexual harassment, understanding the characteristics of various personality types can offer insight on how to help victims prevent, stop, and respond to sexual harassment. This book emphasizes a small collection of information based on research that delivers knowledge in these areas in order to truly prevent and hopefully end sexual harassment.

In addition to understanding the problem, training must provide real solutions rather than the generic: document, report, and move on. This manual looks at real sexual harassment situations holistically and provides solutions for victims, employers, mentors, and the accused. Role-playing is a tried and true method of developing understanding and boosting confidence in handling situations. This book gives role-playing scenarios that are meant to put people face to face with the problem so that they can understand both sides of it and feel more confident in handling it. This is a vital process to learning how to end sexual harassment.

Finally, the book provides a collection of quotes from true stories scattered throughout that reveal the need to end sexual harassment. Although a person could Google sexual harassment cases this year and receive a plethora of results, these stories reveal the difficult situations that have not been solved properly in hopes of offering solutions. The effects of sexual harassment are extremely detrimental, not only to victims but also to the culture that it exists within. Sexual harassment causes hostile work environments and prevents productivity. It can reinforce poverty by preventing victims from being able to work due to mental and emotional consequences. It can prevent education and stifle learning by affecting students. Sexual harassment is harmful to everyone, so everyone's end game needs to be to end sexual harassment.

Sexual harassment is a prominent problem in organizations and institutions. Statistics show that over half of the population have experienced some form of sexual harassment, which demonstrates a need for change. This can start with more effective training.

Part 1: Truly Understanding Sexual Harassment

Chapter 1: Defining Sexual Harassment

True knowledge comes with deep understanding of a topic and its inner workings.
–Albert Einstein

TO UNDERSTAND sexual harassment, it must be examined not only through a generic definition but also through its participants. Most sexual harassment definitions only look at the legal terms, and this indicates that these sources have one goal in mind: to prevent legal issues. This is not a solution to the problem, it is a solution to the organization. But, all organizations have now come to be understood as living organisms that contain a culture. This culture is the people that make the organism thrive. So, to only provide a solution to the organization through the lens of legality is dismissing this culture. It protects the finances or structure, but not the people. Sexual harassment is a people problem, so it involves biological, psychological, and physiological factors. These must all be examined in their relationship to sexual harassment to reach understanding.

The U.S. Equal Employment Opportunity Commission (2017) defines sexual harassment as:

> *Unwelcome sexual advances, requests for sexual favors, and other verbal or physical conduct of a sexual nature constitute sexual harassment when this conduct explicitly or implicitly affects an individual's employment, unreasonably interferes with an individual's work performance, or creates an intimidating, hostile, or offensive work environment.*

This definition fails in addressing the people problem. It does not identify the underlying issues that are important to understanding the problem, nor does it identify the true effects of the behavior. In addition, the language is problematic as it sets the stage for the failings of reports. The language states that the conduct only constitutes harassment based on its effects, which indicates that the effects must be proven. The intangible nature of the effects makes them difficult if not impossible to prove. Also, the term unwelcome implies another need for tangible proof. How does one prove that something is unwelcomed? It is expected that victims will be able to express to the harasser that the behavior is unwanted. Unfortunately, this is not always the case. So, using this definition in training is insufficient in actually understanding sexual harassment.

The underlying cause of sexual harassment is generally identified as a power struggle rather than an actual desire of sex. Why then is power not included in the definitions related to sexual harassment? For instance, why does the definition not include acts that threaten a victim's position or advancement? If sexual harassment is about power, this needs to be included in the language of the definition.

A more sufficient definition of sexual harassment would include the behaviors, the results of these behaviors, the participants, and the causes. In addition, the conduct would not only be linked to affecting or interfering with an individual's work performance or creating an intimidating, hostile or offensive work environment, but it would also be linked to power struggles. Some may argue that intimidating covers the power struggle issue, but this is not necessarily implied. Power struggles can be outside the realm of intimidation. Intimidation is the use of authority or fear to coerce someone. Power struggles can be the use of authority or fear to coerce someone, but they can also be a feeling of entitlement, a need to reinforce a superior role, or a response to a perceived threat.

Perhaps a better definition would be:

Sexual harassment includes any act of a sexual nature that is reported as unwanted. Sexual harassment can include: sexual advances, requests for sexual favors, and other verbal or physical conduct of a sexual nature as these behaviors are inappropriate to the professional environment and may affect the individual's employment, opportunity for advancement, work performance, ability to learn, or create an intimidating, hostile or offensive work environment.

---

* * *

Chapter 2: Who Is the Harasser?

He was nice. He dressed professionally, was clean looking. At first, he just complimented me, so I thanked him. Everyone likes to be complimented. When he told me that he wanted to take my picture, I thought it was something for work. He told me to sit on the desk and cross my legs. At this point, I knew something was wrong, but I was scared to say anything. I thought I had let it go too far.
—Anonymous Contributor

ANYONE CAN BE THE HARASSER. The above example shows that the harasser may be someone you would never suspect. The harasser may be male or female, and may be in an equal or superior role. Although anyone can be the harasser, studies on personality demonstrate some key aspects that should be considered for identification of and understanding harassers. Some harassers may not exhibit these characteristics, personality traits, or motives, but recognizing some of the connections between personality and harassment may allow organizations to be proactive in handling the threat of sexual harassment. This may also give the victim of sexual harassment a new perspective on the motives of harassers. It is important to understand the motives to reach an appropriate placement of blame.

Because power, not desire, is often at the root of sexual harassment, the characteristics of most harassers are centered around the need for power. This is why it is vital to understand the difference between the different forms of sexual harassment. The power struggle form of sexual harassment is usually conducted by those who feel threatened. They are perhaps men who see the gender norms changing and are threatened by women moving into higher positions in the workplace. They are people who may not be strong in their positions and do not want others to surpass them. They may actually have obtained their position out of favor rather than skills, knowledge, and experience, so someone who may have these qualifications would be a threat. The harassment is used to undermine the victim and draw attention away from the harasser's own shortcomings. Although many behaviors can be considered sexual harassment, identifying the root of the problem can be helpful in learning how to overcome it.

I found studies on personality disorders to reveal characteristics that may be associated with sexual harassers. The characteristics may not be exhibited by all harassers, but they are a starting point for identifying the harasser. Personality disorders are different from personality traits. Personality traits are those characteristics that guide how people negotiate the world and respond to external situations and circumstances (Straussner & Lee, 2011). A person can exhibit strong or extreme personality traits without having a personality disorder. Either way, personality has a pervasive impact on work, more than concrete skills or technical abilities (Unterberg, 2003). Thus, personality should be discussed in its connection to sexual harassment. My hope is to demonstrate the need for accurate connections while examining the possible connections.

Unfortunately, studies examining the perpetrators are lacking. Most studies claim that perpetrators are those who fall into the categories above. Little research has been conducted to determine the personalities or characteristics of harassers, which makes recognizing them more difficult. Perhaps the absence of information reinforces the broad variety of harassers. However, psychologists have identified personality disorders that may reveal a link to behaviors conducted by harassers.

Major personality disorders that have been identified to influence certain behaviors which may be associated with sexual harassment include histrionic personality disorder, narcissistic personality disorder, and borderline personality disorder. While people with these personality disorders may not become sexual harassers, some of their characteristics align with those inclined to sexually harass.

Histrionic personality disorder is characterized by exaggerated, dramatic emotions and attention-seeking behavior (American Psychiatric Association, 2000). The characteristics of those who are diagnosed with this disorder are that they are usually sexually attractive, immature, and unable to acknowledge others (Unterberg, 2003). They get jealous, angry and competitive when they are not the center of attention, and they generally seek rewards via provocative behaviors rather than skills (Straussner & Lee, 2011). This disorder is linked to the harasser because the characteristics are representative of those influences on the behavior of the harasser which have been commonly addressed. The feelings of jealousy, anger and competitiveness are all stimuli in sexual harassment.

Another personality disorder that displays a possible link to harassers is narcissism. Narcissistic patients display excessive grandiosity, a need for admiration, a lack of empathy, and exploitation of others (American Psychiatric Association, 2000). They tend to have a desire to attract an abundance of admirers, but while their efforts can lead to strong contributions, these efforts are often directed at self-serving needs for recognition rather than those of the organization (King, 2007, Unterberg, 2003). Subordinates of narcissistic employees feel persistently devalued and inadequate (Cavaiola & Lavender, 2000). This disorder also calls to question the link between these characteristics and those of harassers. There is a need for admiration and a selfish motive. Also, narcissists' ability to make others feel devalued and inadequate demonstrates a strong parallel to the effects of sexual harassment.

Borderline personality disorder patients also have characteristics that may cross over. Individuals with borderline personality disorder exhibit a pattern of intense, unstable relationships, frequent anger, and impulsivity (American Psychiatric Association, 2000). Inappropriate sexual behaviors may lead to claims of harassment (Mentis, 2003). This type of employee needs constant supervision. Being able to recognize this can be a key to avoiding conflicts.

Despite the lack of research committed to the personalities of harassers, an overview of these disorders demonstrates the need for further research and a starting place for identifying characteristics specific to most harassers. The purpose is to change the perspective of sexual harassment. In reports, victims are often viewed as unstable or weak, but the truth is that the problem is the harasser. Something is wrong with someone who uses sexuality, power, or assertiveness against someone. The question is: what is wrong with the harasser? What makes someone harass people? This is the essential part of identifying the problem. Until we understand the problem, it cannot be fixed.

Chapter 3: Who Is the ~~Victim~~ Recipient?

I needed my job. I had kids to feed, and I lived in a small town where jobs were hard to come by, especially jobs that offered good pay and benefits.
—Anonymous Contributor

THE ~~VICTIM~~ RECIPIENT OF SEXUAL HARASSMENT can be anyone. Contrary to many beliefs, victims are not usually targeted because they are weak. In fact, most victims are those who are stronger in character because they pose a threat to the harasser. Unfortunately, this also means that the victims most likely have a lot at stake: they have worked hard to earn their position or ranking; they are supporting a family; they have hopes to advance. Ultimately, the victims are targeted because they challenge the harasser in some way, which indicates that they are either equal to or superior to him or her. Therefore, the term victim has been replaced with recipient.

Recipients of sexual harassment are often blamed for acts of sexual harassment. An attorney who handles sexual harassment claims explained that harassers usually make the recipient appear to be out for money. They will claim that the recipient dressed provocatively, welcomed the attention, and only filed the claim to be awarded. They will dig up information about the recipient's personal life to support their defense, such as financial needs, divorce or relationship issues, and other personal life experiences that may be transposed to benefit the argument. The biggest question then becomes, "Why didn't the recipient report the harassment immediately?" There are many possible explanations for this, but personality is a major factor.

Understanding various recipients' personality traits offers insight on the resistance to reporting sexual harassment. Similar to the studies on the personalities of harassers, there has been little research committed to the personalities of recipients of sexual harassment. Again, this is likely due to the wide variety of recipients. However, personality traits that are common to those who are likely to be recipients can be identified, and they reveal possible solutions to the resistance to report sexual harassment.

Some characteristics of possible recipients include agreeableness, conscientiousness, and openness. The personality traits are exhibited by people who are successful and innovative. Unfortunately, they make people targets for sexual harassment for that very reason. These personality traits are also factors in why recipients of sexual harassment do not report the problem immediately or at all.

Agreeableness is the extent that an individual is likeable, understanding, and diplomatic (Nielsen & Knardahl, 2015). People who are agreeable are more likely to become successful because they are more compassionate, cooperative, trusting and helpful (Nielsen & Knardahl, 2015). In addition, people who are agreeable are also less likely to report sexual harassment immediately because they will either not view the behavior as harassment, or reporting the harassment goes against their nature of being agreeable. Basically, the agreeable employee will not want to cause trouble even if he or she is suffering.

Another personality trait that is highly associated with targets of sexual harassment is conscientiousness. Conscientiousness refers to the degree of organization, persistence and motivation in goal-directed behavior (McCrae & Costa, 1991). Those with this trait are potential targets of aggression due to envy because they are organized and dependable which leads to high job performance (Nielsen & Knardahl, 2015). Harassers may view colleagues with high levels of conscientiousness as threats and seek to undermine their abilities through harassment. Additionally, conscientious recipients of harassment may not report the abuse immediately; instead, they may increase their devotion to their work in order to avoid being associated with malingering or disloyalty (Hoel, Sheehan, Cooper, & Einarsen, 2011). Because they are motivated by work, anything that takes away from their work is negative, and the conscientious person will have trouble dealing with it. They may brush it off and try to ignore it.

People who have high levels of openness will also have trouble reporting sexual harassment. Openness reflects a flexible, imaginative, and intellectually curious approach in dealing with stressful situations (Watson & Hubbard, 1996).

People with this characteristic may feel that they can handle problems like sexual harassment themselves.

No matter which personality a recipient of sexual harassment presents, reporting sexual harassment is not easy. Recognizing that some of these factors may play a role in the reluctance to report is only a starting place for placing the blame correctly. In addition to the already stressful task of reporting sexual harassment, recipients may actually have personality characteristics that prevent them from reporting sexual harassment immediately or at all. Remember that the recipients usually have a lot to lose; combine this fact with personality traits and the difficulty of reporting, and the reluctance to report is clearly explained.

Chapter 4: The Organization

I couldn't report it because I was up for a promotion. If I started trouble, I would be out of the running. Plus, my boss made inappropriate comments all the time, so I didn't feel like anything would be done.
—Anonymous Contributor

THE ORGANIZATIONAL CULTURE plays a major role in sexual harassment. In my studies of business, I have come to understand that organizations are like living organisms. The people function as the parts of the organism, so the nature of the people becomes the nature of the organization. If people within the organization share attitudes that reinforce negative behavior, negative behavior will thrive within the organization. Sexual harassment thrives within organizations that allow sexual innuendos, jokes, and remarks to fly. It also thrives within organizations that reinforce traditional gender roles—having women, no matter their position, do domestic chores like fetching coffee and planning parties while the men are given higher responsibilities.

In order to improve the organization and close the door for the possibility of sexual harassment, two things must be accomplished. First, leaders must make themselves examples.

They must never partake in or allow any inappropriate language or conversations. Second, roles must be divided equally among genders. For example, if there is a need for coffee to be made and this is not someone's designated responsibility, this should be divided equally among women and men.

Changing the organization may seem too daunting a task, which is why there are only two solutions given. These are effective ways to begin to change. Ultimately, the organization as a whole should be one that is innovative in the sense that gender norms are no longer adhered to because diversity is recognized and appreciated. It is the 21st century. Men can make coffee, and if they can't, they should learn how.

Part 2: Solutions

Chapter 5: Why Current Training Doesn't Work By Itself

I had no idea what to do. I told him I was married, but that didn't bother him. He kept on until I had to do something, but I didn't trust anyone at work. So, I saw an attorney.
—Anonymous Contributor

ORGANIZATIONS SHOULD WANT to be the ones to handle a sexual harassment claim because this keeps them from litigation, but if sexual harassment training is insufficient, people often feel forced to seek advice outside of the organization. Training should be cost effective as well as successful. Employees should be able to remember the training and discuss the information so that if they are questioned, it is clear that the training was engaging and informative. If these criteria are not met, organizations face major losses. Also, employees, students, and other recipients deserve to have access to information on how to handle sexual harassment.

You may already know why current training does not work. If you've taken it, you probably do. I said in the introduction that the training that I had been through was a joke. When I was developing my system for sexual harassment training, I examined the problems with that training. I didn't want my training to be a joke.

First of all, sexual harassment videos are outdated and, frankly, insulting. They are more entertaining than informative, which, in this situation, is bad. Now videos may be more convenient because you can reuse them, but they are not effective. People do not pay attention to them. They do not learn from them. And, they usually simply tell people what they already know. They focus more on definitions that real solutions. This can be detrimental for an organization that is truly trying to end sexual harassment.

Second, current training models are not interactive. You know the Chinese proverb, "Tell me, I'll forget; show me, I'll remember; involve me, I'll understand." For something to truly be understood, it must involve participants. People learn best by doing something. Therefore, role-playing is more effective than videos, lectures, etc. Actually placing people in the act of handling sexual harassment will lead to a better understanding of the behavior and how to deal with it effectively.

Finally, current training is not efficiently ongoing. Updating the same ineffective training each year is not really updating anything except for a useless certificate. Environments change, so training should change as well. An excellent example of this is the implementation of social media in the workplace. More and more organizations have realized the benefits of using social media. This was not a thing 10 years ago. There will be more advances in technology five years from now. Social media plays a role in sexual harassment because people may be offended by something shared or an attitude portrayed. Organizations need to know how to handle these situations. This is why sexual harassment training should be updated and ongoing.

The act of doing something repeatedly and expecting different results is insanity. Organizations who continue to implement online and video training for sexual harassment in the workplace are putting themselves at risk. With the shifts that are occurring in this area, organizations must take steps to make better efforts to end sexual harassment.

Chapter 6: Role-Playing

I would tell them to stop, but it would still not work. It was just disgusting.
—Anonymous Contributor

SOMETIMES PRACTICE CAN BOOST a person's confidence in handling a situation. I discovered this when I was preparing for an interview. Having someone role play with me helped me to see how I was handling the questions and how I needed to be handling them. It also made me feel much more confident when I went into the interview. I started using this in my training sessions and instruction, and I saw that it truly made a difference.

Because sexual harassment has many different forms, these scenarios are generic. They should be modeled by a trainer to fit the organization's or institution's needs. Taking a survey and gathering information from individuals can lead to more effective role-playing models. These are just examples. Also, because role-playing is acting out sexual harassment scenarios, parties involved need to sign a waiver stating that they volunteer to participate. No one should be chosen who may be sensitive to the material/acting. However, those who really want to learn how to handle sexual harassment should participate. Role playing is meant to give people the experience of facing a situation as close to real-life as possible in order to build their confidence should they actually face the situation.

Scenario 1: The Subtle Toucher

This scenario calls for two people. One will be the harasser, and the other will be the recipient of the harassment. Others can participate as witnesses. The harasser will initially end a professional conversation by touching the recipient innocently—a shoulder rub.

Explain: This is one of the hardest scenarios to handle because it is confusing. The recipient may not see the act as offensive.

Another conversation takes place, and this time, the harasser puts his or her hand on the waist of the recipient.

Explain: This behavior progresses to the point that the recipient feels uncomfortable and dreads being around the harasser. This often leads to avoidance, self-esteem issues, and lowered productivity. If nothing is done and the behavior continues, the recipient may even quit.

So, how should this be handled?

First, the recipient should understand that he/she is not to blame. Then, he/she should document the occurrence thoroughly. The best means of this is to type up a detailed report of what happened, including time, date, location, and witnesses. If he/she feels comfortable, he/she should tell the harasser that the behavior is unwanted. Script: I do not like it when you touch my waste. Please do not do that anymore. *It is important to recognize that this is simply expressing a feeling that people are allowed to express. It does not make a person a "bitch," "frigid," or a "trouble-maker." People have the right to be appropriately assertive if they feel the need to. Recipients should not feel responsible for the harasser's behavior and should not apologize for not wanting it to continue. If the recipient feels too uncomfortable to confront the harasser, he/she should report the behavior to the designated sexual harassment expert. If the recipient did confront the harasser and feels that reporting the behavior is unnecessary, this is his/her choice. However, if the harasser continues to harass the recipient, he/she must be prepared to report the behavior and explain why it was not reported earlier.

Scenario 2: The Compliment

Everyone likes to be told they look nice, but when do compliments cross the line?

>When a compliment is followed by unwanted behavior, it crosses the line into harassment. Sometimes harassers use compliments to "test the waters." They may also use compliments to set the recipient up. For instance, if the compliment is followed by unwanted behavior and the recipient reports it, the harasser may express confusion because the recipient did not report the compliment.

A compliment also crosses the line when it creates an uncomfortable situation. Sometimes sexual harassment is about how the recipient feels. While many recipients may appreciate a compliment, every experience is different. If a recipient is made uncomfortable by a compliment, this can create a hostile work environment because the recipient may dread coming to work for fear of facing this situation.

This scenario also calls for at least two people. The harasser pays the recipient a compliment: "That shirt looks nice on you." The recipient replies, "Thank you."

Explain: This is a complex situation because on the one hand, it seems that the easiest solution would be to leave personal compliments out of the workplace. However, this poses a problem because it creates a polarized workplace that frankly makes people scared to be nice. Therefore, it is important to establish an environment where compliments can be made and recipients of compliments are allowed to stand their ground when they are uncomfortable by the compliment. While this may seem to put a lot of responsibility on the recipient, if the environment is established, this should ease the tension.

The harasser then compliments the recipient again, but this time he/she adds a blatantly inappropriate comment: "I like those pants. They make your ass look real nice." The recipient responds, "Uh, thanks."

Explain: This begins a pattern of unwanted behavior and leaves the recipient feeling responsible for not handling the initial compliment appropriately.

Solution: When someone compliments you personally, say, "I appreciate compliments, but please keep them professional."

Other solutions: Report the behavior and ask for an intervention. Ask for advice from a sexual harassment specialist or representative. Walk away from a situation that makes you uncomfortable.

These scenarios are just two generic and common ones. The key to successful role playing is to have participants practice responding to harassment so that they feel comfortable facing the problem if it ever arises. Confidence can be gained from repetitive practice.

Chapter 7: For the Recipient

I blamed myself. I quit dressing nice because I thought that I was the reason. No matter what I did, he still kept on. The more I said no, the more he did.
—Anonymous Contributor

I WISH I HAD HAD SOMEONE TELL ME HOW TO DEAL with sexual harassment, but no one that I knew at the time had any real solutions for me. Some people told me to just quit my job, but I felt like that was unfair and unrealistic. Some people told me to hire an attorney, but that was also unrealistic. I needed something else. I really needed two things: 1. I needed someone to make me see that I was not the problem that he was; 2. I needed someone to tell me the magic words to make him stop. What people did not understand was what was going on inside my head.

Society has changed a lot since then, but not entirely. I'm thrilled to see women being more politically active. There is still a long way to go because sexism is deeply rooted in our culture. As I addressed in the first chapter, the language surrounding sexual harassment is problematic and detrimental to the way that it is handled. This is why it is vital for recipients of sexual harassment to understand that the problem is not with them. Dressing nicely, being assertive, exuding sexuality, etc. does not merit someone targeting you for sexual harassment. Remember that sexual harassment 9 times out of 10 is about power and not desire, which means, if you haven't figured it out yet, that your pencil skirt is not the reason you're being harassed, it's your gender that is. Sometimes it's not that the harasser wants to have sex with you. I mean, this may be the case, but if he/she wanted to have sex with you, he/she would go about it in a different way. It is all about shaming you down into a place where your sexuality is seen as something that provokes danger rather than power. That's where the harasser wants you. This is all rooted in the belief that the harassers are powerful and the recipients are not, but the truth is that it is quite the opposite. Recipients do not have to demean harassers in order to move up the ladder. They can do it on their own merit. Hopefully, understanding this will help you see that you are not the problem.

There really are no magic words to make a harasser stop. Sometimes even saying no doesn't work. Sometimes you don't want to say anything because there is such a stigma against being a "bitch" in society. Sometimes you question whether or not the harasser is really harassing you or not. Sometimes you wonder if you are making a big deal out of nothing. You have to value yourself enough to recognize the boundaries that you need to set and stick with them. If something makes you uncomfortable, you should not have to put up with it. You are responsible for your actions, so ask yourself, would I do this? If the answer is no, it's probably harassment. Sometimes you feel like you don't have options. If you cannot quit a job, you have to seek help. You may not know the damage that sexual harassment can have on you until it is too late. Sexual harassment can lead to problems like depression, low self-esteem, low productivity, decreased sexual stamina, and even suicide. Do not let it go that far.

Seek help. Know that you are not responsible for someone else's actions. Be responsible for how you respond. Be accountable for how you respond. Place yourself in someone else's shoes to try to see the situation from a new perspective. If you are in a bad situation, change it. Take care of yourself. You are the only one who can. These are all things that I wish that someone would have told me when I was being sexually harassed. Maybe I wouldn't have suffered debilitating self-esteem, self-loathing, and confidence issues for years if I had just had a little better support.

Chapter 8: For the Organization

I was told I was in a man's world.
—Anonymous Contributor

IF YOU'VE MADE IT THIS FAR, I'm assuming you want your organization or institution to be a sexual harassment free zone, and I commend you. This is a win-win situation because it will increase productivity, loyalty, and confidence in your organization/institution. This is not only about training but also about development. Hopefully, boosting people's confidence in how to handle sexual harassment will also boost their confidence in other areas.

I've already addressed two ways that the organization can make changes, and I'd like to offer two more: 1. Designate a sexual harassment specialist or two. This is important because it frees up the question of who a recipient can report to and get advice from. This specialist will not have to add much to their duties and responsibilities. The specialist may be a human resources professional who is trained but needs to enhance his or her focus on sexual harassment. The specialist can simply do these tasks:

1. Read this book.
2. Read the EEOC page on sexual harassment.

3. Revise the sexual harassment training to include realistic scenarios based on a survey and role-playing.
4. Refresh training every 6 months.

This person should be relatable, respectful of others, and task-oriented. He/she should be available for counseling by appointment.

Have clear sexual harassment policies and procedures. Develop an organizational/institutional specific policy on sexual harassment that aligns with the organization's/institution's vision. It should be clear and concise so that people can understand it. Post the policy in appropriate places. This will help to demonstrate that the organization/institution has taken a stand against sexual harassment, developed a strong personalized policy, and respects its people.

In addition, employees can be given a five-step formula for handling sexual harassment: Identify, Speak up, Report, Know, and Evaluate.

1. Identify the problem and a goal: Write down the incident and include as many details as possible—who is involved, who witnessed it, when it happened, and where it happened as well as the effects. Also, the recipient should determine what he/she wants the result of the complaint to be. This will vary based on the situation. The result can be simply to stop the behavior, or in extreme cases, it can be to remove the harasser.
2. Speak up: If possible, write an email (the best way to communicate a problem) to the harasser. Keep it simple

and concise: Dear _____, On ___(date)___ you __(incident)__. I did not appreciate this behavior. I hope that we can remain professional and courteous without engaging in such exchanges from now on.
3. Report: Follow the organization's procedure on reporting an incident as closely as possible. If you do not feel comfortable reporting to the designated specialist, find someone comparable to report to. Again, use email as this is the most efficient method of reporting.
4. Know what to expect: Two things should happen following the report—the organization should respond to your complaint, and the harasser should respond as well. *This is a very important part of training: training the harasser (alleged) how to respond properly to a complaint as many complaints lead to retaliation which leads to the biggest losses for organizations.
5. Evaluate the outcome: Determine if the outcome is satisfactory or unsatisfactory. If it is satisfactory, be satisfied. If it is unsatisfactory, contact the EEOC.

Conclusion

Sexual harassment has no place in modern organizations and institutions as it only produces negative effects for everyone involved. However, sexual harassment training has not improved for the modern world but rather training has been diminished. Organizations lose millions of dollars each year in sexual harassment litigations. This does not even encompass the effects that sexual harassment has on the culture and reputation of organizations.

This book is only scratching the surface of improvement for training. It is a spark to ignite further studies and the need for change. Hopefully, this spark will turn into an enduring flame that will eventually see the end of sexual harassment.

In order to start making change, training must be personalized and updated. Role-playing is much more effective than lectures, videos, and worksheets. It gives the participants the opportunity to practice saying the difficult things that need to be said in handling tough situations. Doing this will boost participants' confidence in themselves and the organization. Making these suggested changes and demonstrating the desire to eliminate sexual harassment is a step in the right direction for improving the cultures of organizations and institutions.

Recipients of sexual harassment need to stop receiving the blame for harasser's actions. People are only responsible for their own actions. Harassers are responsible for their actions, not recipients. End of story.

I chose not to focus on technical definitions and statistics because I wanted this book to be accessible, and that information can be easily found online. I wanted the focus of this book to be the problems with training, solutions for those problems, and new perspectives on sexual harassment. My hope is to change the way sexual harassment is handled in order to end this problem.

References

American Psychiatric Association. (2000). Diagnostic and Statistical Manual of Mental Disorders (4th ed., text revision). Washington, DC: Author.

Cavaiola, A.A. & Lavender, N.J. (2000). Toxic coworkers: How to deal with dysfunctional people on the job. Oakland, CA: New Harbinger Publications, Inc.

Hoel, H., Sheehan, M., Cooper, C. L., & Einarsen, S. (2011). Organisational effects of workplace bullying. In S. Einarsen, H. Hoel, D. Zapf, & C. L. Cooper (Eds.), Bullying and harassment in the workplace. Developments in theory, research, and practice (2nd ed., pp. 129–148). Boca Raton, FL: CRC Press.

King, G.K. (2007). Narcissism and effective crisis management: A review of potential problems and pitfalls. Journal of Contingencies and Crisis Management, 15(4), 183-193.

McCrae, R. R., & Costa, P. T. (1991). Adding Liebe und Arbeit: The full 5-factor model and wellbeing. Personality and Social Psychology Bulletin, 17, 227–232. doi:10.1177/014616729101 700217.

Mentis, L. (2003). My life's a mess and it's all your fault! Employee Relations Law Journal, 29(1), 68-82.

Nielsen, M. B., & Knardahl, S. (2015). Is workplace bullying related to the personality traits of victims? A two-year prospective study. *Work & Stress*, 29(2), 128-149. doi:10.1080/02678373.2015.1032383.

Straussner, S. L. A., & Lee, D. (2011, January). Identifying and treating employees with personality disorders. *The Journal of Employee Assistance*, 41(1). Retrieved from http://go.galegroup.com.libraryresources.columbiasouthern.edu/ps/i.do?p=PPPC&sw=w&u=oran95108&v=2.1&it=r&id=GALE%7CA352492000&asid=a870e2708d8ce2d3fc6d3d0de64cbe0f.

U.S. Equal Employment Opportunity Commission. (2017). Facts about sexual harassment. Retrieved from: https://www.eeoc.gov/eeoc/publications/fs-sex.cfm

Unterberg, M.P. (2003). Personality: Personalities, Personal Style, and Trouble Getting Along. In J.P. Kahn & A.M. Langlieb (Eds.), Mental health and productivity in the workplace: A handbook for organizations and clinicians (pp. 458-480). San Francisco, CA: Jossey-Bass.

Watson, D., & Hubbard, B. (1996). Adaptational style and dispositional structure: Coping in the context of the five-factor model. Journal of Personality, 64, 737–774. doi:10.1111/j.1467- 6494.1996.tb00943.x

THE END GAME

www.ingramcontent.com/pod-product-compliance
Lightning Source LLC
Chambersburg PA
CBHW020714180526
45163CB00008B/3078